Write Up a Storm
Storm
WITH THE
Polk Street School

YEARLING BOOKS/YOUNG YEARLINGS/YEARLING CLASSICS are designed especially to entertain and enlighten young people. Patricia Reilly Giff, consultant to this series, received her bachelor's degree from Marymount College and a master's degree in history from St. John's University. She holds a Professional Diploma in Reading and a Doctorate of Humane Letters from Hofstra University. She was a teacher and reading consultant for many years, and is the author of numerous books for young readers.

A Polk Street Special

Write Up a Storm
Storm
WITH THE
Polk Street
School

Patricia Reilly Giff
Illustrated by Blanche Sims

A YEARLING BOOK

Published by
Dell Publishing
a division of
Bantam Doubleday Dell Publishing Group, Inc.
1540 Broadway
New York, New York 10036

ISBN: 0-440-40882-2

Printed in the United States of America

Book design by Christine Swirnoff

November 1993

10 9 8 7 6 5 4 3 2

To
James Patrick Giff,
Christine Elizabeth Giff,
William Langan Giff,
and our 1993 Thanksgiving baby,
with love

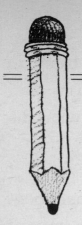

Introduction

I come from a family of storytellers.

My grandmother loved to talk about her trip down the Delaware River. Eyes flashing, arms waving, Nana told me about her escape from alligators, barracudas, and a parrot that stole her red hat.

On Sundays my mother and her sisters told stories too.

Sometimes they'd tell them at the same time.

I'd have to pick which one to listen to . . . and sometimes I could go back and forth and make a new story about what the three of them said.

I too loved telling stories.

Nana listened seriously as I told her about the kidnapper hiding in the garage, my cat who knew sign language, and the horse who lived in my closet.

I wanted to write the stories down. I wanted to be a writer.

I didn't know how though . . . I didn't even know how to begin. And when I did put a few sentences down on paper, I was afraid to show them to anyone. Suppose someone laughed at the sad parts or didn't laugh at the funny parts?

So I stopped trying.

I didn't begin again until I was grown up.

I'm sorry about that.

If I could live my life over, I'd write from the time I learned to put two words together.

It's a joyous part of my life.

I want that joy for you too.

We all have stories to tell, and from the moment we begin to talk we want to share them.

So this book is for you, to help you on the way, to show you anyone can write a story.

I've tried to think about exactly how I do it.

Each chapter tells you the steps I use.

It's not very hard . . . not if you practice.

I hope you'll try.

I'll look for your name in print.

1

Take a Person

Anyone can write a book.

You need paper.

Stacks of it.

You need pencils.

I like them as pointy as Sherri Dent's nose.

But more important, you need a living-room floor.

Whenever I begin a book, I sink down on my blue rug and close my eyes.

Fiddle, my cat, knows I'm writing, or maybe he thinks I like catnaps too. He drapes himself around my neck like a black-and-white fur collar and begins to purr.

The sound of it always helps me think. It reminds me of the snips and bits I've saved in my mind for a story.

It reminds me of the day I began the Polk Street books.

I was in New Jersey, talking with kids about writing.

A boy came up to me. He yanked on my arm, hard. "Hey," he said. "Write a book about me."

"Hey," I answered. "What's your name?"

He thought for a moment. "My name is Richard." He looked around at his friends. "But don't call me that. Call me 'Beast.' That's what everyone calls me."

Beast.

Perfect.

I looked at him carefully to make sure I'd remember.

His freckles.

His hair standing up in front.

His striped T-shirt and jeans.

I wondered what was in his pocket. A crumpled-up homework assignment? A nickel? Maybe a smooth, dark stone?

Later, lying on my rug with Fiddle, this is what I think about: a boy named Beast who fools around and laughs a lot.

I have to add something that will make him different.

How about his teeth?

Maybe he still has baby top teeth.

He'd hate that.

But wait a minute.

I could use a girl in this story too.

I sit up straight. Fiddle slides down to my

lap. My daughter is in the kitchen. She's making cookies, eating the chocolate chips instead of stirring them into the batter.

"Alice," I call.

Fiddle stops purring. He wonders why I want her. Maybe to bring me a snack? Fiddle loves potato chips, the saltier the better.

But I don't ask Alice for food. I ask if she'd like to be in a book.

She comes to sit on the floor with me. "Sure," she says. "I'll be the star."

I smile, thinking about Alice.

When Alice was in second grade, she loved to wear red sneakers to school.

She had Popsicle legs and scabs on her knees.

She'd reach into her closet, pull on a pink party dress with chocolate stains on the collar, and think she was a TV star.

It's fun to think about what might be in

her pocket. A tube of Chap Stick she pretends is lipstick? A small rubber unicorn called Uni?

"Pick a name," I tell her now. "Not something that begins with B."

B is Beast's first letter.

We need to set the names apart so the reader won't be mixed up.

Together we choose Emily.

A last name is harder.

I have scraps of paper with names all over the place. Names of people I meet, like Adrianne Turnipseed and Charlie Nightingale.

Names from mailboxes like Tracy Matson.

Names from gravestones like Gideon Gregory.

It's too much trouble to look through all of them though. The telephone book is easier.

I found the name Valentine Casey in a

telephone book once. I flipped it over to make Casey Valentine. I loved that name. I used it in one of my first books, *Fourth-Grade Celebrity*.

For some reason, Alice and I start at the back of the phone book. That's why it takes so long to find the right name. When we do, it almost jumps out at us.

Arrow.

Emily Arrow.

A friend for Beast.

We don't even have to search for Beast's last name. The name Best pops into my head.

It's just right.

Down on the floor there are a few other things I'll do. Fun things. Easy things.

I'll give Beast and Emily their own families.

I noticed something a while back. I usually have only two children in a family. Beast will end up with an older sister. Emily will have a younger one. I wonder why.

I think it's because I have only one sister. I guess we write about ourselves.

I know this too: As I write, something will happen to Beast and Emily. They'll change and grow.

After a while he won't be the boy in New Jersey. She won't be my daughter Alice.

They'll be themselves.

But that's the way the story begins.

It begins with a person or two.

What they look like.

What their names are.

That's almost all I know.

That's the way I begin.

You can begin that way too.

CAN YOU SEE HOW I DID IT?

This is the way I showed the people in *The Beast in Ms. Rooney's Room:*

Beast: *He was probably the only kid in the whole world who still had baby top teeth.*

Emily: *She had on a pink party dress and dirty red sneakers. Her legs looked like Popsicle sticks.*

Matthew: *He had stick-out ears and a wet-the-bed smell.*

Here's Sherri Dent in *The Valentine Star:*

Her tongue was as pointy as her face.

And in *Rat Teeth*, Cliffie looks in the mirror and sees himself:

He looked like a vampire. Even when he closed his mouth, the ends of his two front teeth stuck out like little white tombstones.

YOUR TURN . . .

Pick a person.

Give him a name: a first name and a last name.

Tell what she looks like. Can you see his face . . . what he's wearing?

How does he act? Is he serious . . . does he worry all the time? Is he funny . . . jumping around . . . always in trouble?

Do you know what's in his pocket?

Think about him. Dream about him.

Make sure you like him.

That's the first step.

Put Him in
a Place . . .

It's breakfast time.

I put two bowls of cereal on a tray.

My desk and typewriter are upstairs, waiting.

It's nice to have a place to write, your own place.

I used to write in a closet. It was small and cozy, with a little window for spying. I missed it when we moved away.

But I've written in other places too. The

corner of the garage. The laundry room. Perched on a wide windowsill.

I know a girl who has a terrific place to write. She slides under her bed, shoves out her shoes, the dustballs, and her collection of shells. She loops up the bedspread so she can see, but no one knows she's there.

Find yourself a place too, an everyday place, a place to leave your paper and pencils and notes.

The spot I have now is an old bedroom.

Fiddle the cat loves it.

As I go up there with the cereal, Fiddle is one step behind me.

He climbs on the desk and starts in on the green bowl of Krispies. I take the yellow one.

Fiddle eats fast.

I eat fast too.

The milk flies all over the place.

I know he wants to finish his cereal ahead of me and help me with mine. He looks over every once in a while to see if he's beating me.

He isn't.

Fiddle spends half his life in the woods, fooling around with spiders and slugs. I like to keep his dirty nose out of my cereal.

While I eat I think.

I still don't know where the story happens.

I look out the window. I can almost see Beast and Emily dancing in the glass.

Where are they dancing?

I push the tray back, still wondering about a place for them.

I lean forward. What I see outside is Fiddle.

How did he tiptoe out there in the blink of an eye?

He did it while I was thinking about my book people. He took one padded step after another, down the stairs, pushing the screen door open with his little wet nose.

He's chasing birds again, of course.

I tap on the window.

He flicks his tail. "Don't bother me."

This cat is evil as a snake. I race out, waving my arms around. "Watch out, sparrows!"

I grab him just in time.

He looks up. "I was only fooling," he seems to say.

I go back to Beast and Emily, dumping Fiddle on a pillow as I pass the bed.

Where are they? What's a good place for them?

Then I have it.

I take them by the hair of their imaginary heads and drop them into a place I know.

School. The school where I taught.

My school.

I'll use this same school for all the Polk Street School books.

I know what the classrooms look like, the halls.

I know the principal. He's kind and funny and loves to play ball.

I even know that miserable substitute teacher. The one with the fat stomach and the little skinny legs. The one who yells all the time.

It's such a neat feeling when I decide on a place for my story.

It's always a real place . . . so the whole thing is laid out for me.

Once I tried to write about a place that wasn't real. It was for a mystery called *Have You Seen Hyacinth Macaw?*

In Chapter One, Abby Jones's bedroom was green. In Chapter Two, it was blue.

Abby followed the criminal down Lumber Street in Chapter Three. The same street was River Road in Chapter Four.

It was a mess.

I had to keep going back to try to find what I had made up.

What I made up was my mind. I decided I'd always write about a place I had seen, a place I knew well. My house. My neighborhood. The place where my husband grew up.

We have a little cottage on a river in New York. I tucked it into *The Girl Who Knew It All*:

It was probably the smallest town in the whole round world. There was only High Flats Road,

which started at the bottom of Hubbell Moun-
tain and ended at the river. In between there
were fourteen houses, seven on each side of the
road. Tracy's was stuck on the end closest to the
river . . .

Whenever I go somewhere, I look around carefully. I want to remember it for a story.

I check out the pictures on the walls and the books in the bookcases. I memorize the lamps and the color of the couch.

To be a writer you have to look at things like these, everyday things, in a new way.

Pretend you have a magnifying glass.

Look sharply at the bits of dirt in the anthill on your front path. Put what you see into words. How does the hill look to you? How will it look to your story person?

Do the same thing with the chairs in your

kitchen. Can you see the scratches on the legs? The gravy stain on one of the seats?

I always mean to get a notebook to write down those details. I tell kids to get notebooks too. I forget though.

Instead I write on bits of paper. The same kind of paper I use for saving names. Papers float from the top of the table and drift under the couch.

When company comes, I throw the scraps out and start over. But I remember a lot of those places anyway.

Try it yourself.

CAN YOU SEE HOW I DID IT?

Here's Matthew's place. It's his new house in *Matthew Jackson Meets the Wall:*

Matthew closed the bathroom door, leaned against it, and looked at the walls. Pink wallpaper fish were swimming around in circles. Blue bubbles were coming out of their mouths.

Matthew tried a couple of spit bubbles in the mirror. . . .

He took the steps down two at a time, raced into the kitchen, and looked around.

Instead of fish blowing bubbles there were tan coffeepots all over the wallpaper. Tons of them.

The coffeepots were tipped over, pouring brown coffee into tan cups.

The countertops were tan and so were the cabinets.

"Yuck-o," he said.

YOUR TURN . . .

Think of places you know.

Find one for your person.

Let us see what the house looks like . . . or the school.

Splash on some color: Paint the walls, wallpaper the kitchen.

Take us outside to see the yard, the gray squirrel in the tree, the bike in the garage.

Don't forget to collect places for other stories.

Give Him a Problem

Suppose you read a story about a boy in school. He had lots of friends. He did all his work. He had good marks. Nothing went wrong for him.

Lucky boy.

Boring story.

Suppose instead that something is missing in the classroom. Maybe someone's money. Suppose this boy was in the classroom alone. Maybe everyone will think that he stole the money.

He has a problem now. A big problem.

Wouldn't you want to read about him?

That's the way a story works.

Something has to happen to your story person—something that will worry him, a problem that he will have to solve.

This problem has to be interesting.

It has to make the reader wonder . . . what's going to happen next?

I think that finding the story problem is the hardest part for the new writer.

Until it gets easier here's what to do.

Get out that pile of paper I talked about in the first chapter.

Have you ever had a problem?

Write it down.

Ask your friends about their problems too.

That's one thing about problems. Everyone has one.

To find a problem for Beast I wrote down all the things that bothered me in school.

My best friend, Francis McHugh, moved away.

I hated science . . . and eating in the cafeteria.

These problems didn't seem just right for a boy named Beast.

And Beast's problem had to be a big one, big enough for the reader to worry about too.

After a while I got sick of trying to find one.

It was just too hard.

Maybe I should take a walk, I told myself. I could take a quick trip to Baskin-Robbins.

I could have a praline ice-cream cone with peanut-butter cups.

Or . . . I could go to the beach. I saw a purple jellyfish floating in the shallow water the other day. I picked up a pearly-pink shell.

Stop.

This is what happens to writers when they get stuck. They think about all the things they could be doing instead of sitting on a hard chair at a messy desk.

Does that happen to you?

You have to take a deep breath.

You have to tell the cat you are definitely not going to play with him.

You have to close your eyes and think.

Where was I?

A problem for Beast—and I'm not going to move until I find one.

Maybe he's sick.

No, not Beast.

Maybe he can't find his homework?

Yes, that would be Beast, but this problem won't last long enough for a whole book. It's not big enough for a whole book.

I keep thinking about the homework though.

I keep thinking about Beast getting into trouble.

He might be late to school.

Yes. But it has to be more than that too.

He might hate school. Yes. Good idea.

"Go away, Fiddle. I've almost got the problem."

What would be a really big problem for a kid who hates school . . . who's late . . . who forgets his homework?

It's so easy I don't know why I didn't think of it sooner.

He's been left back.

That's a huge problem.

A problem that's big enough to write a whole book about.

That's just what I'm going to do. I won't get off my hard chair. I won't leave this messy desk.

It's a relief to find a story problem.

I remember trying to find problems for my other books.

I wrote about a boy who had a terrible day once, and all the things that went wrong for him.

I wrote about a girl who wanted to be important, and felt she was only a lump of vanilla pudding.

I wrote about a boy who was a clumsy baseball player, but wanted to be part of the team.

Problems are all over the place once you

begin to look for them. They're right in front of your nose!

Let me help you find one.

Suppose your person's best friend has moved away, and he has no friends?

Suppose your person has moved away? He still wouldn't have any friends.

Suppose he's lost his cat . . . or his dog has run away?

Suppose he's going to run away.

You could keep going forever.

Don't though.

Just choose one.

CAN YOU SEE HOW I DID IT?

Here's Richard Best/Beast's problem:

First he thinks about it . . . *Last year they [the rest of the class] were babies in Mrs. White's class.*
Now they were in Ms. Rooney's class.
And so was he. Again.
A left-back.
The kids probably thought he was huge. Gigantic. He slid down in his seat. He pulled his head into his neck a little.

Then, to make it worse, the other kids talk about it. . . .

Kevin Klein shook his head. "You're not in our class anymore." He looked as if he felt sorry for Richard.

"By a mistake," said Richard. "By accident."

"By dumbness," Drake said.

YOUR TURN . . .

Give your person a problem.

Not a little one that can be solved in two minutes or even an hour.

A big problem.

Something that interests you. Something that will interest your reader.

The closer it is to a problem you know something about, the better it will be.

Make sure it's something you'd worry about if the problem were yours.

Make sure it's something your reader would worry about too.

Got one?

Now you're ready to write.

Make Him Move . . .

I don't mean make him move away.

I mean make him move around.

Is there anything worse than just sitting still?

Not much, in a story.

A reader wants to follow the main character from place to place.

A reader wants *action*.

And moving is action.

The action I was thinking about that Monday morning was just to put a piece of paper into the typewriter . . . and to find out what had happened to Fiddle.

That cat.

We had finished breakfast while I was thinking about the most important sentence in the book. The first sentence.

An action sentence.

The sentence that would make the reader dive into the story.

Was I paying attention to Fiddle as he slid out the front door? Of course not.

Now I had to find my sneakers. The old ones with the holes in the toes. They were the only ones fit for where I was going.

I sped outside, down the back path, and into the woods.

I called him for ten minutes.

Did he listen? Probably.

Did he answer? No.

I went back into the house, yanked off my sneakers, and sat at my desk.

I needed the first few sentences.

Moving sentences.

Action sentences.

The hardest sentences in the book.

I felt like a juggler.

Today the book was beginning, the writing part.

On the first few pages I had to show the person.

I had to show the place.

I had to show the problem.

I had to hook the reader in.

This was going to be a school story, so I'd start in school.

I began to write.

The nine-o'clock bell rang. Richard Best pounded down the hall of the Polk Street School.

Yes, Beast would pound down the hall. He wouldn't just walk.

That's another thing I collect. Action words.

Scribbled over bunches of pages are words like *racing* and *running, dashing* and *jumping*.

Once I spent a morning figuring out how to get a person to sit down.

I wrote:

> *Tracy Matson sank down on the bench in front of the office.*
> *Tracy slid into her seat.*
> *She slumped down on the floor.*
> *She collapsed into the chair.*
> *She fell onto the soft pillows.*
> *She perched on the edge of the stool.*

There are a million ways to show action, but you have to find exactly the right way for the person you're writing about.

Beast and Emily are fun to write about because they're always hopping around, always into a mess.

It was much harder to write about Grace in *The Gift of the Pirate Queen*.

Grace was quiet, she was worried, she was sad. So I wrote about her moving this way:

Slowly she turned Willie [the goat] around and led her back to the pen.

She followed Willie inside and set the bowl down next to her. Then she snuggled into the hay to watch as Willie nosed into the cereal.

She could feel a lump in her throat. Everything was going wrong. She shivered and curled up a little closer to Willie.

You can see how slowly Grace moves, how quietly. You know that she doesn't race or dash or throw herself from one chair to another.

And speaking of moving, what do I see out the window right now? Fiddle. He's marching along the stone wall at the side of the house.

Something is dangling from his mouth.

I close my eyes.

I didn't see that, I tell myself.

That was not a mouse swinging back and forth.

A dead mouse.

I pull the typewriter closer and try to think about Beast.

Richard burst into Room 113.

Not so hard.

Not as hard as watching a killer cat on the loose.

If I can do it, you can too.

CAN YOU SEE HOW I DID IT?

Here's some action . . . some of Beast's, of course. You can recognize him by what he does, even if you don't see his name.

He frowned at her. Then he pulled in his breath. Sniffing loudly, he stuck the eraser end of his new pencil up his nose.

He shook his head. The pencil swung back and forth gently.

The girl looked as if she were going to throw up.

Good.

YOUR TURN . . .

Start your story off with a bang!
Use action sentences.
Moving sentences.
In a notebook, or on a couple of scraps of paper, begin an action-word list. Make it fun . . . make the words jump across the page.

Make Him Talk

It's hard to find a problem.

It's hard to make a person move.

But the best part for me, the part that's the most fun, is the talking part . . . the part writers call *dialogue*.

In the beginning I had to find out just how to do it.

So I read . . .

I went to the library, took fifteen books, and dumped them on the table.

I should have been quieter about it, I guess. I could see the librarian frowning at me.

I sat there reading a page from one book, a paragraph from another.

I saw some things I liked, some things I didn't.

I noticed that you have to put quotation marks around anything someone says. This tells the reader someone is talking. For example:

"Who's been eating my potato chips?" I asked.

"Meeee-owwww," said Fiddle.

Another thing. Writers begin a new paragraph every time a person finishes what he's saying, and every time a new person begins to speak.

Matthew took a huge bite of pizza. "I love this," he said.

"Close your mouth, Matthew," Cindy said. "You look like a cement mixer."

Matthew closed his mouth. He waited for her to look at him again. Then he opened his mouth wide and shut it.

"Gross," Cindy said. "The grossest thing I ever saw."

I like making new paragraphs like that. They're short and perky. The page looks good, and the book gets finished faster.

I also like the way writers use the word *said*. It slides into a sentence like Jell-O on a spoon.

No one even notices *said*. It just lets us know quietly who's speaking.

Those writers who use words like *exclaimed* or *cried* or *hissed* draw attention to the word itself, instead of to what's happening.

I learned to stick with *said* and *asked*.

I learned to save the big words for once in a while.

Something else: the talking, or *dialogue*, has to sound as if someone were really saying it. Play with the words. Read them aloud.

Sometimes my words sound awful to me. I know real people would never talk that way.

When that happens, I tuck a notepad into my pocket. I close the door behind me carefully, so Fiddle can't follow, and go down the front path.

From the window I can feel Fiddle's eyes on my back, glaring at me. He wants to go to the park.

He loves the park.

He loves to listen to the kids talking as much as I do. He loves to rub up against their ankles.

I sit on a bench, in the shade, and listen to what they're saying.

That's the great part about being a writer.

You can be as nosy as you please.

If someone says something about it, just raise your eyebrows. Tell him, "This is what a writer has to do."

Sometimes it works. Most of the time it doesn't.

Anyway. Listen to the way people talk.

They don't talk in long sentences that take forever to say.

They talk in pieces, little fragments like . . .

Beast flew down the hall.
"Those are school pants?" a voice said.

He looked up. It was Mrs. Kettle, the strictest teacher in the school. "Just because it's summertime . . ." she said. She shook her head.

Beast looked down at his jeans.

There were long strings hanging from the hole.

"I didn't know . . ." he began. "I forgot that . . ."

One last thing about this talking business: Everything that is said has to do with the story.

You can't just talk about the weather unless the weather's important to the story.

You don't want to talk about what your person ate last night or where he went last week.

Stick to talking about his problem!

CAN YOU SEE HOW I DID IT?

In *Beast and the Halloween Horror*, Beast has told a lie. A big lie. He knows he's in trouble.

> *"I knew it," Holly said. "You've got tears in your eyes."*
>
> *"The leaves are flying all over," he said. "One got in my eye."*
>
> *"You'd better tell me, Richard." Holly sighed. "It's terrible to have a brother who's a troublemaker."*

Beast closed his mouth. He wasn't going to tell Holly one thing.

"Come on, Richard," she said.

"You'll tell Mom," he said.

"No I won't," she said. "I promise."

YOUR TURN . . .

Take a new piece of paper.
Make your person talk to:

   his mother
   his teacher
   his friend
   his enemy

Let him tell you about his worries.
Read the paper aloud.
Make sure the person sounds like himself
. . . the person you picture in your mind.
Now put him back in the story.
Let him tell about his problem.

6

Make Him Worry About the Problem

Worry. That's what always happens to me when I get halfway through the story.

Something stops. Everything stops.

Does it happen to you?

You're going along as fast as you can, the words almost pouring onto the page.

Then suddenly the pen moves slower, or the typewriter doesn't click along.

You can't think of anything to say.

It always happens. What is it?

And what do you do?

First a warning: Never, never throw the story away. Never.

I go to the refrigerator . . . Fiddle's favorite place after the potato-chip closet. I pull out something to eat.

A writer has to eat.

You can tell your mother that.

I chomp down on a piece of something and calm myself.

Then I try to think about what's wrong.

(Yes, Fiddle is chomping too. I don't know if he cares what's wrong.)

At this point someone will ask, "Did you make an outline of your story?"

"Absolutely not," I'll answer. And you can answer the same thing, if you wish.

I know some writers, and some teachers too, who like outlines. They enjoy making

A's and B's, I's and II's. And when they're finished, the story is laid out like a map.

You might try to outline. It might be easier that way.

I can't make it work for me though.

If I outline, my story is boring. Nothing unexpected happens along the way. A person doesn't pop up and say, "Hey, I'm here too. I'm fun and important, and I want you to do something with me."

But back to the middle-of-the-story slowdown. Suddenly my people don't dance in my window.

They sit on the edge of the page, frowning at me, not moving, not talking.

What I think happens is that I have to backtrack. There are things about the story people I haven't thought about . . . things about their problems I have to learn.

That might happen to you.

Here's what I check. You might want to do the same thing.

First take a good look at your person.

Can you see him? Can your reader see him?

If not, go back to the living-room floor and make him real.

Think about that magnifying glass again.

Look through it at your person's face.

See that face clearly, sharply. The color of his eyes, the thickness of his hair.

How white are his teeth?

How big are his ears?

Does he talk softly or loudly?

Does he laugh a lot?

Look inside his head. What are his thoughts and feelings?

Right now you might discover something.

The story person may not look like you, but the story person's thoughts and feelings are yours.

Yes, I am like Emily.

She has a little sister who's funny and sings a lot, and you can tell that Emily really loves her. My little sister, Annie, was funny too. She sang all the time. And, of course, I have a special love for her too.

And Beast? I'm even like Beast.

The things that worry Beast and Emily are the things that worry me.

Beast is worried about being left back.

Now, I have to tell you I never was left back. But I know a couple of kids who were.

And I would really be worried if it happened to me.

In another book Beast is afraid to climb the gym ropes.

I was not afraid of the gym ropes—I was

terrified of them! I could never, ever climb to the top. Even thinking about it makes my hands wet.

So it was easy to make Beast worry about that.

In *Pickle Puss*, Emily wants to win the library contest.

So did I.

It was hard not to cheat, hard not to add in some books I hadn't read, so I knew exactly how Emily felt.

Now here you are, down on your blue rug, or your brown rug, thinking about yourself as the story person, and what you're afraid of.

You take a look at the problem.

Does the problem really worry you, really scare you?

If your person doesn't solve it, would you feel terrible?

Talk to yourself.

No, you're not weird. All writers talk to themselves.

Then tell yourself it's usually one of two things that make the story stop: a person who's not real or a problem that doesn't make your person worry enough.

Which one is it?

Maybe it's both.

Maybe you'll have to go back to the beginning and add or change things.

Oops. I just remembered something I should have told you before.

When you're writing, make sure you leave lots of room between each line. If you type, use double spaces. If you're writing on lined paper, leave every other line blank.

When you need to go back, it's easier to put things in between.

You don't want to keep writing pages over and over.

Your hand might fall off.

But you do need to fix, to cross out and do over. Rewriting makes your story smooth. It makes it live.

CAN YOU SEE HOW I DID IT?

Watch Richard/Beast worry in *Purple Climbing Days:*

Richard closed his eyes.

Climbing day.

He had forgotten all about it.

He was supposed to climb the rope in the gym.

Climb it to the top.

He didn't even like to climb the monkey bars.

"Today I'm going to grab that rope . . ." Matthew began. "Today I'm going right up there."

Richard put his books in his desk.

Today was the day he was going to fall off the gym ceiling. He was going to break his neck.

YOUR TURN . . .

Is your person worrying about his problem?

Worrying enough to make the reader worry too?

If not, go back.

Reread.

Do you care enough about what happens to your person?

Is his problem really big enough?

If you have to change anything, do it now.

And the Problem Gets Worse and Worse

A bird is in my house.
   Really.

It's a little brown one, a song sparrow.

It flew down the hall into one of the bedrooms.

I didn't see it at first, but I did hear the sound of its wings.

I shoved back my chair, wondering.

Then I saw Fiddle's long black tail, disappearing into the doorway.

This cat is getting worse and worse, I think.

He must have caught the bird, and the poor thing escaped in the living room.

I'm after them in a flash. A moment later I'm standing with one foot on a chair, the other on a dresser top.

Fiddle looks up at me.

I guess he thinks I'm catching the bird for him. He thinks it's his prize.

"No good," I say, and scoop the bird into a soft towel.

Outside, the sparrow skitters to safety in the andromeda bush and smooths its feathers.

I think Fiddle needs a bell on his collar. As soon as I work out today's writing problems, I'll walk to the pet store to buy one.

A brass bell for his yellow collar.

Back to Beast.

I'm now into the middle part of the book. I call this part Making the Problem Worse and Worse. Some people have another name for it. They call it *plotting*.

Whatever you call it, it means keeping the reader wondering and worrying. What's going to happen next? It means making every page so interesting that the reader can't wait to turn to the next one.

So now I have to make Beast's problem worse and worse. Sometimes it's hard to do. I have to play games with myself.

All writers play the What if . . . game.

It goes like this.

What if Beast is left back? What if he'd have to see all his old friends playing ball without him? What if the school bully makes fun of him?

Then if Beast tells everyone there's been a mistake, that the teacher has mixed up the records . . . the kids will know he's a liar.

Yes, it's getting worse and worse for Beast . . . and more exciting for the reader.

That's the What if . . . game. You could even call it the Plotting game.

You've probably played it a hundred times.

Play it a hundred more times.

Think of a What if . . . game on the way home from school.

Try one while you're brushing your teeth.

It's what writers do to create excitement . . . excitement for the story person . . . excitement for the reader.

It works a little like an old cartoon I remember. Did you ever hear someone say, "He's painted himself into a corner"?

In the cartoon you can see someone painting the floor.

He backs up as he paints.

Instead of backing out the door he backs himself into a corner.

What's he going to do now?

If he walks across the newly painted floor, he'll ruin it.

He'll have a mess of paint on his sneakers too.

He has to think of a way to solve the problem.

But he can't.

He's painted himself into a corner.

And that's what you're going to do.

Paint your story person into a corner.

Even you can't think of a way out.

CAN YOU SEE HOW I DID IT?

Matthew, in *Matthew Jackson Meets the Wall*, starts out with one problem. He's moving to a new house, and he's sad about that.

But now the problem is worse: His cat has run away.

And even worse: He's afraid of the boy next door . . . a big, strong boy called "the Wall."

"Listen," Matthew said. "Barney's missing. Maybe she's trying to get home."

For a minute Beast didn't answer. . . . "Matthew, what's the matter?"

Matthew shook his head. His eyes were watering. "Nothing." He took a breath. "There's this kid. He's strong as an ox. He's after me."

". . . Listen," Beast said. "Stay in the house."

"Forever?" Matthew said.

Just then there was a click in the phone. "I've got to hang up." Another click. "Look for Barney," he yelled. . . .

Matthew put the phone down. He could almost see Beast running over to his old house. . . .

It wasn't his old house anymore. It was someone else's.

YOUR TURN . . .

It's time to make the problem worse and worse.

Each time the reader starts a new chapter, your story person is in more trouble.

Play the What if . . . game.

Paint your person into a corner.

Pile his troubles up as high as you can.

And in the End . . .

You solve the problem.

No, not you.

The person in the story solves the problem.

His mother can't do it for him, nor can his father.

Even his friends must stand back and watch.

The most any of them can do is help . . . just a little bit.

It is his problem.

He has to solve it.

He has to get out of that painted corner all by himself.

It's hard.

What's he going to do, all painted up like that?

At this point I call Fiddle. "Come on," I say. "We're going for a walk."

He comes along, of course.

He doesn't exactly walk with me.

I think he doesn't want to look like a baby.

He marches ahead about half a block. Once in a while he looks over his shoulder to make sure I haven't disappeared.

I hope the neighbors aren't watching me.

I'm talking to myself in a loud voice. "Then what . . ." I say. "What does my story person do?"

Matthew Jackson took the first step to solving his problem for me. I didn't expect it to happen this way, but suddenly Matthew was . . .

> . . . *sick of being a coward, sick of being afraid. He started to walk, moving faster [toward the Wall]. No more coward, he told himself.*
>
> *He was almost running now.*

At last Matthew is going to do something about his troubles. He's going to face the Wall, no matter what.

But sometimes it's not so easy. I've spent a long time getting the problem to get worse. I can't fix it in two minutes.

So I walk . . . sometimes for a couple of days.

One thing helps in trying to figure out the end.

Something important has to have happened during the book.

The person has been changing, growing.

"Wait a minute," you say. "My person hasn't changed. He hasn't grown one bit. He's the same old person I started out with."

Take out your story and read it again.

Do you mean to tell me that, with all the problems he's had to worry about, he hasn't gotten a little wiser?

I hope he has.

I'll bet he has.

And this will help you end the story.

Let me tell you about Beast.

Remember how much he hated being left back?

He's gotten himself into one mess after another.

Trouble in school.

Lying.

But then . . . then he learns he's been causing some of his own trouble.

He can stop running in the halls.

He can do the best he can.

And now his problem is solving itself.

It was the same way in *Purple Climbing Days*.

At the end Beast won't climb the rope all the way to the top.

But he begins to believe in himself . . . to believe he can do what he has to do.

So maybe your person won't solve his problem completely.

Maybe he'll begin to solve it.

And that's enough, if he's changed and grown.

That's all you can expect.

The reader will finish the last page and be satisfied. The story has ended in a way that feels right to the reader, that feels good.

And that's what makes a writer happy.

CAN YOU SEE HOW I DID IT?

Here is Richard/Beast in *Purple Climbing Days*. He has worried about climbing that rope. He's had some help from Mrs. Miller the killer, the substitute teacher. He's had a little practice. He's learned something about being brave from the classroom skink, a tiny lizard who lives in a tank.

Now in the end Richard has to be brave too. Here he goes . . .

> *"Climbing day," said Emily.*
> *"I can do it," said Richard.*
> *. . . Richard went to the rope. "Half-way," he told Mr. Bell.*

"Good start," said Mr. Bell.

Richard grabbed the rope. It felt rough against his hands.

He thought about Mrs. Miller.

He thought about the skink.

He darted his tongue in and out.

Then he began to climb.

YOUR TURN . . .

It's time to make your person do something.

He has to solve his problem.

Take a walk.

Think about what he might do . . . what seems right for him to do.

If you don't want to walk, pick up a pencil.

Write down all the things you can think of to solve his problem.

One will click.

Sooner or later.

But you'll solve it . . . I promise.

9

And Now . . .
Start on Page 1

Take a deep breath.
   You're finished.
Oh no you're not.
You're coming to the best part.
Have you ever been to the beach . . . picked up a shell that was smooth and polished . . . without a sharp edge in sight?

That's what you're going to do to your story.

Sometimes you have to wait a few days.

Sometimes you're so sick of thinking about your story, looking at your story, that you can't even tell what's good about it . . . or what's bad.

So take a little time off. That's all right.

Look at the story on a Saturday morning when it's sunny and you feel happy. Or pull it out on a snowy day when you can snuggle on the couch.

Sharpen your pencil.

Read the whole thing aloud.

Do you love your story person?

Can you see his place clearly . . . or do you need to add a sentence or two so the reader can see it?

How about that problem? Big enough?

Are you happy with the way it's solved?

Every sentence in the whole book has to belong. Every word that everyone says has to be about the story.

And speaking about words . . . Get rid of the old tired ones. *Very* is one. *So* is one. How about *but* and *though*? Make a list of some of the ones you're sick of . . . and remember not to use them yourself.

Check those sentences too . . . Do they drag on forever, strung together by *and*? Make believe you have a scissors, and snip them down to the size of a comfortable breath.

It's your last chance to listen to the words. Make sure they're the strongest, the boldest, the most colorful.

And then, at last, you're really finished.

But Wait a Minute . . .

Yes, wait a minute.

I just thought of something—another story. Maybe you thought of it first.

Fiddle is a great story person.

I can see you frowning. Of course he isn't really a person.

But I've made him seem like one.

I've given him thoughts and feelings.

And it would be fun to write about his Life Saver–green eyes, his long black tail.

He's evil as a snake, and everyone loves him.

Especially me.

I don't even mind that he chomps down on my toes when I move them in bed.

A person.

Yes.

And he has a place too. From the writing room to the woods outside, to the rug on the bottom of the stairs that he's chewed to pieces. (When company comes, I have to cut the strings with a scissors.)

So his place is easy.

What about a problem for him?

He doesn't have a problem.

He has a perfect life.

He must know what I'm thinking. He stares up at me. His green eyes are slits.

So what's your problem, Fiddle?

Me?

I'm his problem?

I won't let him chase the sparrows, the robins?

I'm stingy with the potato chips?

There was the time I caught him all the way down at the end of the road.

I could almost picture him carrying a suit-case.

Was he moving out?

That's a good beginning for a story, more than enough to start.

Do you want to try it?

Go ahead.

You can have this. I don't mind.

There are so many things to write about.

You just have to start.

CAN YOU SEE HOW I MIGHT DO IT?

• Chapter 1 •

Fiddle rushed down the stairs.

He waited for the door to open.

Then he sneaked out.

He pulled his long black tail after him just in time. "Mm-rrrr-ow."

The door slammed shut in back of him.

Good.

He was never going back . . . not even if

that woman dumped a hundred potato chips in his bowl.

He was going to run away. Now. This minute.

Everything was wrong. Everything. . . .

YOUR TURN . . .

You know how to do it:
First you take a person.
Put him in a place.
Give him a problem.
Make him move.
Make him talk.
Make him worry about the problem.
And the problem gets worse and worse.
And in the end you solve the problem.

AND YOUR TURN AGAIN . . .

I love to see my books when they're finished. You can see yours finished too. Use the next pages to make your own book.

Here's what you'll need:
    scissors
    glue or paste
    a stapler
    masking tape or cloth tape
    Scotch tape
    wrapping paper or wallpaper

Here's what to do:
1. Cut the pages carefully on the dotted lines.

2. If you think you'll need more pages, use a blank piece to trace an extra one on plain white paper.

3. Copy your story in your best hand-writing . . . or ask someone to type it for you. You can also illustrate it with your own pictures.

4. Don't forget a wonderful title, and a dedication to someone who is important to you.

5. Stack the pages together and number them in order.

6. Staple them together on the left-hand side.

7. For a cover, cut two pieces of cardboard, one for the front, one for the back. Make the pieces a little larger than the book pages.

8. Tape the pieces together with one piece of masking tape or cloth tape.

9. To finish your cover, find pretty paper, gift wrap perhaps, or wallpaper. The paper should be two inches longer than the book. It should be much wider: double the size of the book plus two inches.

10. Center the cover on the paper and fold each corner of the paper in and tape it to the book with Scotch tape.

11. Next, fold each side in and tape to the book with Scotch tape.

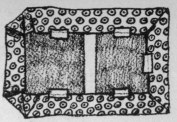

12. Use one piece of cloth or masking tape to tape the pages to the front cover and another to tape the pages to the back cover.

13. Cut a piece of gift wrap or wallpaper that is twice as wide as the pages of your book and just as tall. Fold it in half and glue or paste one side to the front cover and the other to the first page. Take another piece of

paper the same size and do the same with the last page of the book and the back cover.

14. Write the title on the front cover, and your name underneath.

15. Enjoy sharing your book with your friends . . . and don't forget to start a new story tomorrow.

_____

_____

By

_____

Dedicated to

_____

Chapter ____

Chapter ___

Chapter ____

The End